THE FOUNDATION

THE FOUNDATION

Its Place in American Life

Frederick P. Keppel

With a new introduction by
Ellen Condliffe Lagemann

Transaction Publishers
New Brunswick (U.S.A.) and Oxford (U.K.)

New material this edition copyright © 1989 by
Transaction Publishers, New Brunswick, New
Jersey 08903.
Originally published in 1930 by the Macmillan Co.

All rights reserved under International and Pan-
American Copyright Conventions. No part of this
book may be reproduced or transmitted in any form
or by any means, electronic or mechanical, including photocopy, recording, or any information
storage and retrieval system, without prior permission in writing from the publisher. All inquiries
should be addressed to Transaction Publishers,
Rutgers–The State University, New Brunswick,
New Jersey 08903.

Library of Congress Catalog Number: 88-24923
ISBN: 0-88738-239-8
Printed in the United States of America

Library of Congress Cataloging-in-Publication Data

Keppel, Frederick P. (Frederick Paul), 1875–1943.
    The foundation: its place in American life/
    Frederick P. Keppel with a new introduction
    by Ellen Condliffe Lagemann.
        p.   cm.
    Reprint. Originally published: New York:
    Macmillan, 1930.
    Bibliography: p.
    ISBN 0-88738-239-8
    1. Endowments—United States.   I. Title.
AS911.A2K4 1989
011.4′4—dc19   88-24923
                                                    CIP

INTRODUCTION TO THE TRANSACTION EDITION

Frederick Paul Keppel was president of the Carnegie Corporation of New York for nineteen years, from 1922 until 1941. The Corporation, which was chartered in 1911, was the last of the various philanthropic trusts established in the United States by the steel magnate Andrew Carnegie. Its endowment was large—$125 million in 1911 (to which $10 million was added after Carnegie's death in 1919)—and its mandate was broad: "to promote the advancement and diffusion of knowledge and understanding." As its president, Keppel became a widely respected interpreter of philanthropic foundations. *The Foundation,* which was first published in 1930, was one of his best-known works. Composed of talks he had given as the Page-Barbour Lecturer at the University of Virginia, the book provided a brief, straightforward, and frank discussion of foundations and their activities. At a time when relatively little was known about such organizations, the volume was rightly praised as "well worth reading" by those "who would keep acquaintance with important social factors."[1]

What did *The Foundation* have to say? It began with a review of the history of foundations and then went on to explain the current organization of the Rockefeller Foundation, the Carnegie Corporation, the Julius Rosenwald Fund, and a number of other trusts. It set forth the purposes and procedures of different types of foundations—community foundations such as the New York Community Trust as well as such grant-making foundations as the Commonwealth Fund. Comparing foundations to universities, the book argued that the most essential common purpose of all types of funds and foundations was the furtherance of learning, culture, and research. Beyond such generalities, the book offered comments that, according to Keppel, made it "a good deal more advisory than ... intended" (p. 93). Thus, it argued that the ideal foundation executive should "practice ... the art of being well-informed" (p. 93); and that informal advisory boards should be relied upon to provide specialized expertise. Obviously, there was considerable accuracy in the review headline that read: "Now You Can Know the Foundations."[2]

In addition to being informative, the Keppel vol-

Transaction Introduction vii

ume was noteworthy for the candor of its observations and criticisms and for the sensitivity and humility with which problems of foundation administration were treated. Keppel need not have recounted the major findings of the (U.S.) Commission on Industrial Relations, which argued that foundations were little more than extensions of the corporate influence of their donors, but he did. What is more, after noting that there had not been a similarly hostile investigation for fifteen years, he pointed out that it was a moot point whether this was "due to the presence of wisdom on the part of the foundations... or to the absence of knowledge and interest on the part of the public" (p. 30).

In line with the above, Keppel also included in the conclusion to *The Foundation* the sage observation that "as believers in democracy, we are bound to look forward to the day when the community will take over the functions now performed by the foundation" (p. 110). Whether he was suggesting that in a more thoroughly democratic society than the United States was in 1930, there would be no need for organized social assistance, or, alternatively, that in a more thoroughly democratic society, such large concentrations of money and power would not be tolerated, was not clear. Still, from a man who was so closely identified with foundations, the observation was forthright, to say the least.

Sprinkled throughout the text of *The Foundation*, there were, in addition, a variety of comments and allusions that clearly indicated the degree to which the Carnegie Corporation's president was able to empathize with applicants for foundation funds. Typically, Keppel noted that "no matter how trivial any proposal may seem to another, it is never trivial to the person making it" (p. 67). And, typically too, he worried about "the number of really gifted people who do not fit into any scheme which would bring them to the favorable attention of existing foundations. Some generous person willing to take a chance might create a foundation to look after just such cases," he observed (p. 40). However practical the suggestion, it conveyed the thoughtfulness and concern that were characteristic of Keppel. Indeed, if *The Foundation* was most interesting at the time it appeared for the insight it offered into the actual daily management of philanthropic trusts, it may be most interesting in retrospect as an introduction to a man who played a significant role in the history of foundation philanthropy in the United States.

Genial, urbane, fun-loving, and generous, Frederick Keppel was a person of great integrity and character. "Notwithstanding his love of people and his gaiety," a lifelong friend observed, he "had a high, stern Scotch-Irish covenanting spirit."[3] Consistently intelligent and sometimes wise, Keppel was more all-embracing in his thought than profound. His interests were wide-ranging. An associate once wrote that "the most powerful spring that animated him was an eager, ceaseless concern to educate himself in everything that related to man in his time. He was the exact contrary of a specialist."[4] Not only that, his greatest interest was people and his greatest gift an unusual capacity to appreciate human nature. Widely known as "FPK," he was affable, charming, and held in great affection by a great many people. As a *New York Times* editorial put it soon after his death in 1943, he was "the kindliest and most indulgent of executives... [and] able to get loyal service from everyone who came under his spell. Sometimes he was disappointed in projects that didn't pan out. But hopefulness radiated from him. With a gently humorous appreciation for human frailities he loved humanity."[5]

Keppel was born on Staten Island in 1875 and reared in New York City and its environs. He graduated from Columbia College in 1898, and spent most of his pre-Carnegie Corporation career as a Columbia administrator and dean. He left Columbia in 1918 to assist Secretary of War Newton D. Baker in Washington. After World War I, he might have liked to have become a college president, but he was not able to find that kind of job. More from default than from choice, he therefore agreed in 1922 to become president of the Carnegie Corporation. It was a fortunate decision for all involved.[6]

Once austere, formal, and forbidding, under Keppel's leadership, the Carnegie Corporation became a friendly, hospitable, lively, and fast-paced place to work. Although he kept the staff small, Keppel hired young secretaries and assistants to replace the former associates of Andrew Carnegie who had worked there. Although he expected everyone to push themselves as hard as he pushed himself, he inaugurated the still-continuing tradition of a four o'clock tea, at which he personally presided—"very definitely a family affair," a colleague recalled.[7] The volume of correspondence received at the Carnegie Corporation was considerable, but, to the extent possible, Keppel tried to answer all letters himself. He even set aside fifteen-minute appointments for as many of the people who asked to see him as could be fitted into a crowded day. According to John M. Russell, one of his assistants, "FPK's office was the most informal and friendly in the business."[8]

The administrative routines that Keppel introduced into the Carnegie Corporation were coupled with grant-making practices that featured the wide distribution of a large number of often small grants—"scatteration," he called it. To be sure, Keppel was asked by the Corporation's trustees to develop grant programs featuring such areas of priority interest as adult education and the fine arts, which he did. But grants within these programs were extraordinarily diverse, and, since as often as not, major grants did not fall within these programs, they really did not give focus to the corporation's granting of funds. Beyond that, the relation of one grant to another technically categorized as fitting within the same program was rarely self-evident and even more rarely explicated in a clear and sufficient way.

Keppel knew that efficient organization was not his strong suit and that he thought, wrote, and acted in an essentially divergent, ad hoc way. Although the context was different, with typical candor he wrote in *The Foundation:*

> Please don't look for logical sequence in the discussion of foundation policies upon which I am about to embark. It isn't there. I've tried the different sections in half a dozen different orders without success. With so many different questions of principle arising in connection with the making of any particular grant, and so much to be said

on both sides, I am consoling myself with the thought that perhaps the best way for you to grasp the many difficulties of the situation is precisely through the feeling of complexity and confusion which I am sure my treatment of the matter will furnish. (pp. 34–35)

Such apologies notwithstanding, his "inclination to disperse benefactions widely" was irksome to some trustees. One critical member of the Corporation's board lamented, for example, that "a trustee sometimes had the feeling that he was sharing in the conduct of a retail business involving more particular transactions than he could classify or understand." Furthermore, when pressed to explain why some proposals warranted support and others did not, Keppel would say, "I have to play by ear and proceed by 'hunch.' I can't work otherwise."[9] Whatever strains this style created, Keppel still remained the dominating figure at the Corporation throughout his long term in office. As one trustee explained it, "the Board pretty generally did what Fred said."[10] For almost twenty years, therefore, the granting of Carnegie Corporation funds was guided more by Keppel's innate generosity and sense of people and things than by formally articulated principles or policies.

There were obvious disadvantages to this. In *Funds and Foundations*, Abraham Flexner claimed, for example, that in the domain of adult education, which was of special interest to Keppel, his "procedure in handling [grants]... was doomed from the start. He assumed too great a responsibility and operated over too extensive an area."[11] Although Flexner's comment had merit and may have had application beyond one program, it is also clear that Keppel's preference for "scatteration" and his informal style made many friends for the Corporation. Even if he was less systematic in his orientation than some would have liked, and even if he did not foment fundamental changes within a limited domain, as Flexner did, for example, in the domain of medical education, many people admired what a *New York Times* editor described as "the various highly intelligent ways of doing good which he has worked out for the Carnegie fund."[12]

To have thus won trust, respect, and goodwill was not an insignificant accomplishment. At the time Keppel became president of the Carnegie Corporation, "the foundation" was still a relatively new type of philanthropic organization. Even though the Peabody Fund was established in 1867, it was not until the early years of the twentieth century that John D. Rockefeller, Andrew Carnegie, and other men and women of enormous wealth began to establish the trusts that would come to be known collectively as "the big foundations."[13] Hence, in 1922, the public still had relatively little knowledge of foundations, and what knowledge they did have tended to be colored by pre-World War I, progressive distrust of monopolies, trusts, and robber barons. Although the point cannot be proven precisely, it seems likely that Keppel helped to change this. His administrative style and his effort to find the money necessary to assist as many seekers as possible would have been likely to help remove the distance, mystery, and, in some quarters, hostility that had surrounded foundations. One could have faulted Keppel for many things, but one would have been hard put to describe him as malevolent or ideological.

As president of the Carnegie Corporation, Keppel was, of course, in an unusual position to communicate not only with a public made up of the increasing numbers of people who had received Corporation funds or otherwise had direct contact with the foundation but also with other philanthropists. From the first, Corporation presidents had assumed the role of exemplar and instructor to their peers. Certainly this had been the case of Andrew Carnegie, who had personally served as the Corporation's first president. From the time his famous essay, "The Gospel of

Wealth," was first published in the *North American Review* in 1889, until his death in 1919, all Carnegie's philanthropic acts had had a didactic intent. Three men followed Carnegie in the Corporation's presidency before Keppel's appointment: the lawyer Elihu Root (1919–20); the psychologist James R. Angell (1920–21); and the president of the Carnegie Foundation for the Advancement of Teaching, Henry S. Pritchett (1921–23).[13] All three wanted the Corporation to be exemplary among foundations, and urged their brethren trustees to identify and support causes that would enable the foundation to engage in trend-setting patterns of giving. Accepting this corporate sense of responsibility for philanthropic leadership, Keppel spent a good deal of time lecturing, consulting, and writing about "the foundation." He believed that foundations were accountable to the public for the care and intelligence with which they administered the monies deeded to them. And he hoped that as they began to open increasingly their doors and books to outsiders, they would be subject to constructive rather than destructive scrutiny and criticism.

To what extent other philanthropists heeded Keppel's call for openness and a service orientation is difficult to know. But it does seem likely that some of his practical suggestions—for example, the suggestion that foundations publish annual reports—and, even more, his equation of responsibility with public candor, set a standard for the field. After all, Keppel was personally admired by many people, and the foundation he presided over was one of the giants in the field. Both factors would have been likely to have encouraged acceptance of his ideas.

In the end, then, what can one say of Keppel's accomplishments as president of the Carnegie Corporation? Although the outcomes of the grants authorized on his recommendation were as varied as the grants themselves, Keppel addressed himself consistently and effectively to questions of foundation responsibility, accountability, and indeed, legitimacy. Via the policies and practices he instituted at the Carnegie Corporation, and via his advice to others, he tried to enhance the standing of "the foundation" as an agency of public policy-making and public service that could represent the interests of the community as a whole. And he seems to have had considerable success in the effort. Foundations gained in public esteem during the interwar years, which, not coincidentally, were the years of his presidency. Indeed, those decades were notable for the absence of a major congressional investigation of foundations.

What is more, even though it was neither clear, certain, nor inevitable early in the twentieth century that foundations would gain enduring public acceptance, by the 1940s that had happened. They had become familiar, if sometimes controversial, institutions. Their existence was accepted by the public, and they had defined the procedures needed to justify the assertion that they were professionally managed organizations and not private associations dominated by a wealthy donor or that donor's family. Keppel understood what had to be accomplished for foundations to gain an established place in American society and quietly but importantly contributed to the processes through which that was achieved. *The Foundation* is helpful in understanding how and why he did what he did.

Notes

1. Charles Cecil Smith, Review of *The Foundation*, by Frederick P. Keppel, *Social Science* 6 (1931): 328.
2. William McAndrew, "Now You Can Know the Foundations," *School and Society* 32 (1930): 611–12.
3. R.C. Leffingwell, "Postscript," in *Appreciations of Frederick Paul Keppel by Some of His Friends* (New York: Columbia University Press, 1951), 123.

4. Lewis Galantière, "France after the First World War," *Appreciations*, 38.
5. "Frederick Keppel," editorial, *New York Times*, 10 September 1943.
6. There are two biographies of Keppel: David Keppel, *FPK* (New York: privately printed, 1950), and *Dictionary of American Biography*, s.v. "Keppel, Frederick Paul."
7. John M. Russell, "Inside FPK," *Appreciations*, 74.
8. Ibid., 75.
9. Henry James, "President of the Carnegie Corporation," *Appreciations*, 58–59.
10. Leffingwell, "Postscript," *Appreciations*, 122.
11. Abraham Flexner with Esther S. Bailey, *Funds and Foundations: Their Policies Past and Present* (New York: Harper & Brothers, 1952), 123.
12. "Frederick Keppel," editorial, *New York Times*, 10 September 1943.
13. The phrase is from Waldemar A. Nielson, *The Big Foundations* (New York: Columbia University Press, 1972), which presents a very different portrait of Keppel in the chapter on Carnegie philanthropy.
14. Although Keppel was elected president in 1922, he did not actually begin full-time work until 1923.

INTRODUCTION

The selection of "The Foundation—Its Place in American Life" as a title to be included in the honorable sequence of Page-Barbour Lectures has been based on four reasons. First, frankly, my own deep interest in the subject; second, my faith in the essential importance of the foundation as a factor in American progress; third, in spite of this importance, the very general ignorance on the part of the public regarding foundations; fourth, the University and the State in which I am to speak, for in many ways the relationships of the foundation with the South has been particularly close.

My own interest is personal and, in view of Andrew Carnegie's large responsibility for the whole movement as we see it today, it may also be said to be *ex officio*.

In support of my second reason, I might cite the uniform willingness of our most distinguished citizens to serve on foundation boards, or the judgment of thoughtful observers from other lands where foundations have not developed as they have in the United States. Or I might offer specific examples of what foundations have actually accomplished, and this I shall try to do as we proceed. Most of the modern instances of activities upon which I shall call are from Carnegie trusts, because these come first to my mind, but equally representative examples could be selected from other foundations.

I think I could demonstrate the weight of my third reason, the prevailing ignorance about foundations, if I should at this point look up from my manuscript and begin to ask you questions. There are today more than two hundred foundations, with an aggregate capitalization of almost a billion dollars. How many of you could give the correct title and stated purpose of half a dozen of them? I hasten to add that this ignorance is not limited to the academic public, but frequently includes people eager to reap the benefits of foundation grants, and sometimes even those directly concerned with foundation activities. It almost looked as if the community was not only ignorant but content to remain so, when discussion following the recent announcement of the Julius Rosenwald Fund and the conditions of its charter gave evidence of a more widespread interest.

As to the relations with the South, it is my belief that the better economic conditions which are giving us a new South full of dynamic possibilities for the future are not in themselves the underlying cause for the change, but are the result of advances in education and in community health, both of which, as you all know, are due in large measure to foundation activities, notably those of the General Education Board and the Rockefeller Foundation. It is interesting to recall also that one of the largest nineteenth century American foundation gifts, the Peabody Fund, was made by a Northerner for the benefit of the South, and one of the largest and most important of the twentieth century gifts, the Duke Foundation, is also for the South, but given by a Southerner. The South is also the center of the present activities of the Rosenwald Fund, to which I have already referred, and of a number of smaller but influential organizations such as the

Phelps Stokes, the Jeanes and the Slater Funds.

In what I shall have to say about foundations, it is only fair to point out that the opinions expressed are my own; others equally entitled to pass judgment might not agree as to matters of emphasis and might heartily disagree with some of my most cherished conclusions. Indeed, frankness compels me to add that in certain preliminary discussions this has already proved to be the case.

CONTENTS

	PAGE
INTRODUCTION TO THE TRANSACTION EDITION	v
INTRODUCTION	xix
PLACE OF THE FOUNDATION IN THE GENERAL PICTURE OF PROGRESS	3
PAST AND PRESENT	15
FOUNDATION POLICIES	33
ORGANIZATION AND PROCEDURE	61
FOUNDATION ACTIVITIES	77
CONCLUSION	93

THE FOUNDATION

THE FOUNDATION

PLACE OF THE FOUNDATION IN THE GENERAL PICTURE OF PROGRESS

As generally understood today, a foundation is a fund established for a purpose deemed "charitable" in law, administered under the direction of trustees customarily operating under State or Federal charter and enjoying privileges with respect to taxation and continuity of existence not accorded to "non-charitable" trust funds. The fund is to be used for a designated purpose, broad or narrow as the case may be, the donor specifying whether the principal is to be kept intact or whether not only interest but principal may be spent for the purpose named. Though the practice is not uniform, it is the tendency to designate the former as Foundations and the latter as Funds. Individual donors, or their lawyers, have thought of interesting variants. One-fifth of the income from the present Duke Foundation, for example, is to be set aside to "snowball" until the original capital of $40,000,000 is doubled.

4 The Foundation

As to the distribution of capital, there is again a wide range. In some cases, though permission is given, it was evidently the intent of the donor that it should be used only in emergencies. In other cases, the donor deliberately looked forward to the distribution of capital, but left it to his trustees to determine the most desirable rate of distribution. Mr. Julius Rosenwald has, on the other hand, specified that his Fund must be disbursed within twenty-five years of his death, and Senator Couzens has made somewhat similar provision in the case of the Children's Fund of Michigan, recently endowed by him. The Falk Foundation of Pittsburgh is following suit. In two recent cases the trustees have decided, rather than to make any extended use of the income, to effect an immediate distribution. The trustees appointed by the late Payne Whitney, instead of creating a foundation, as they might have done under the terms of Mr. Whitney's will, announced the immediate distribution of the principal sum entrusted to them, amounting to nearly twenty-six million dollars, among certain institutions in which Mr. Whitney had already shown an interest and had supported with characteristic generosity. An even more recent example was the distribution of the Hubert Fund by a Board of Trustees consisting of Calvin Coolidge, Alfred E. Smith, and Julius Rosenwald.

Much of the endowment of our colleges and universities, and the same is becoming true of hospitals, museums, and other public institutions, is legally in the form of separate foundations, the trustees, however, being the trustees of the institution in question and the objective taking its place in the general program of the institution. We also find cases of semi-detached trusts, as, for example, in the relations between the Mayo Foundation and the University of Minnesota, or between the Yenching Fund and Harvard University.

What we normally have in mind in speaking of a foundation, however, is the independent institution, not the one in which the responsibility of the trustees is secondary to their interest in a larger unit.

The Director of the Twentieth Century Fund, Mr. Evans Clark, has recently performed a useful service in analyzing the activities of one hundred and eight such foundations in the United States and displaying in graphic form their capitalization, their methods of operation, and their fields of action. Some of them, I fear, are foundations only in name, but the list includes all the important legitimate trusts. Although there is of necessity considerable duplication, his classification as to foundation activities is nevertheless instructive: individual aid, forty-eight; education, thirty-six; scientific research, thirty-three; child welfare, twenty-six; health, twenty-two; social welfare, eighteen; international relations, three; æsthetics, nine; industry and business, seven. Twenty-nine more are divided among sixteen other designated fields.

With these varied purposes in mind, let us make one more elimination before we really get to our subject. The purely charitable trusts, important as they are as evidence of the spirit of human brotherhood and in view of the individuals whose lives are made happier thereby, are of less significance to the community than the foundations whose purpose is constructive rather than palliative and which have to do with educational, scientific and social progress.

Its Place

American foundations range in financial resources from a few thousand dollars to nearly $200,000,000, and in purpose from some objective of more than parochial narrowness, as, for example, to provide the services of a brass band upon the anniversary of the donor's death, all the way to the promotion of "the well-being of mankind throughout the world." Six of these foundations, whose purpose is general rather than specific, have an aggregate capitalization of five hundred and ninety-six million dollars, and these have already contributed from income alone more than two hundred and eighty million in the last ten years. While these figures seem large when stated thus baldly, they are relatively small. The aggregate endowment of all American foundations is estimated to be less than half of what the American people contribute for philanthropic purposes in any single year, and hardly more than one per cent of the total national income.

By the terms of the gift some foundations, like the Buhl, at Pittsburgh, are local in scope, some, like the Duke, are regional, some national, and some international. Most have come into existence as expressing the will of a single

The Foundation

The foundation is a spender only, whereas the university both spends and earns. Instead of a central location, the work of the foundation may be scattered over all the world. The Carnegie Institution, for example, owns and operates thirteen different and widely distributed properties for scientific research.

And yet to me, at any rate, the similarities seem more important than the differences. It is an interesting coincidence that the aggregate endowment of our foundations and of our colleges and universities is approximately the same —about one billion dollars, though the property of the latter is, of course, much larger. The responsibilities of the trustees, both in the control of finances and in the general direction of activities, are the same. In both, important decisions are based on group rather than individual judgment and derive their significance from this fact. Almost without exception permanent foundation executives have had their training in universities. Dr. Pritchett was called to the Carnegie Foundation from the Presidency of the Massachusetts Institute of Technology, and the Rockefeller Foundation called successively President Vincent from

Its Place

the University of Minnesota and President Mason from the University of Chicago. Furthermore, whenever a foundation needs temporary help, it turns uniformly to the university.

It is only natural that the relations between the two have always been close. The foundations have learned by experience that one of the most satisfactory ways of disposing of their burdens of responsibility is to lay them upon the universities as operating agencies, sometimes in the form of general endowment, more often as time goes on, for specific purposes mutually agreed upon. The experience of the university, on the other hand, is constantly bringing to light opportunities for the foundation in the form of enterprises which no institution could carry through unaided, but from which all institutions and all communities might profit.

At one time it looked as if a new type of operating organization—the separate research institution—would absorb an increasing share of foundation funds. The Rockefeller Institute for Medical Research had achieved a world-wide renown, and shortly after the war a number of independent institutes in economics and other related fields were established, largely through foundation aid. A more recent tendency, however, certainly so far as endowment grants are concerned, is for the foundation to pin responsibility upon the university as the agency having the greatest assurance of permanence and bearing furthermore a recognized responsibility to a broad constituency for its standards and its activities.

Clearly, there is the greatest variety alike in the size, the purpose, the organization, the program, and the geographical range of American foundations; we are far from agreement as to the most useful form or organization or as to the most fruitful type of program. But all this is, of course, as it should be, since the ultimate basis of the utility of the foundation as an instrument of progress will probably rest upon this very diversity.

PAST AND PRESENT

PAST AND PRESENT

The endowment has its roots deep in human history. With a fine sense of alliteration, my colleague, Dr. Furst, to whom I am indebted for much of what I am about to tell you, points to Plato's endowment of the Academy, the Ptolemys' of the Library of Alexandria, and the younger Pliny's of a school in his native town. The idea of permanent provision for worthy purposes fitted admirably into the ideals and practices of the Christian Church, and from the fourth century until the Reformation, practically all endowments were Church endowments. English endowments were thereafter related more particularly to the City Companies of London. Toward the end of the eighteenth century some men began to doubt the social wisdom of tying up funds in this manner. The basis of Turgot's criticism was that the donor "cannot communicate his own zeal from age to age," and Adam Smith's that "the effect of endowment on those entrusted with any cause is necessarily soporific." The foundation is not without criticism today, although the basis of the criticism is not the same. These current doubts and fears will be dealt with later on.

Adam Smith's forebodings were in considerable part justified by the report of the British Charity Commissioners, created in 1860. Though the report showed the general record of the City Companies to be good, there were a number of cases where presumably practical men had permitted serious impairment of capital and grave misuse of funds.

Since its organization this Board of Charity Commissioners has exercised a wide supervision over trusts and endowments, and has been particularly useful in releasing funds which could no longer carry out the stated purpose of the donor, as in the case of the fund devoted to helping the victims of the Barbary Pirates. It may be noted that across the Channel, the French Republic, originally perhaps because of its critical attitude toward the Church, has exercised a most minute scrutiny over foundations, and that this is probably the reason why there are so few foundations in France, and why their rôle is comparatively unimportant.

Past and Present

Foundations, of course, come only from surplus wealth, and therefore one cannot expect to find many examples in the early history of the United States. Some that we do find are of importance. Benjamin Franklin's two bequests of one thousand pounds each to the cities of Boston and Philadelphia, have had an eventful history. In 1803 came the first social service endowment, the White-Williams Foundation being established in the interest of "unhappy females who were desirous of returning to a life of rectitude." The next mile-post was set not by an American, but by an Englishman, James Smithson, who in 1846 bequeathed $508,000 to an American foundation, the Smithsonian Institution, "for the increase and diffusion of knowledge among men." The Peabody Fund of more than $2,000,000, created in 1867 and closed in 1914, has already been referred to.

In spite, however, of the very great interest and significance of some of these earlier grants, the American foundation is distinctly a twentieth century phnomenon, only seven of any importance having carried over from the nineteenth.

This being in very broad outline the background, what are the factors which brought about what may be called the boom in American foundations in the early years of the twentieth century?

One can, of course, only guess at the reasons for the creation of any specific foundation. The donor may not be averse to the publicity attending his gift. He may not be blind to the conveniences attending exemption from taxation. He may desire to perpetuate his own name or that of some one dear to him. He may be, and he often is, genuinely and intelligently interested in the objects the foundation is to serve. But the dominating reason, I am sure, is the recognition of "the stewardship of surplus wealth." A sense of stewardship alone, however, would not account for the greatest of these gifts. They represent a faith in man and in his possibilities for progress which lies deeper than the sense of stewardship. These two qualities were united in the heart of Andrew Carnegie, and it would be hard to overestimate his influence in the development of American foundations. *Triumphant Democracy* was published in 1886, and *The Gospel of*

Wealth in 1900. The first of his American foundations was created in 1896. No less influential than the soundness of his precept and the magnificent generosity of his example were, I am sure, the vibrant personality of the man and particularly the infection of his enthusiasm.

He would, however, have been the last to claim more than his share of the credit. With the growth of American prosperity, the obligations of stewardship were also recognized by others, but were not at first reflected in the creation of foundations, but rather in gifts, sometimes of princely generosity, to agencies more familiar to the public and to the donor. I have in mind such examples as the founding of a memorial university by Senator and Mrs. Leland Stanford in 1891, and the re-creation of the University of Chicago by John D. Rockefeller in 1892. Mr. Carnegie's letters give more than a hint of the influence upon himself of Charles Pratt's establishment of Pratt Institute in Brooklyn and Enoch Pratt's library gifts in Baltimore.

Two happenings outside our own country must have had their influence also—the creation by Cecil Rhodes of his Trust in 1902, and the publicity which it received in the United States through the selection of American Rhodes Scholars, and to a lesser degree the widespread interest in the Nobel Prizes, also awarded by a foundation, established in 1890.

From the day when what he called in his Autobiography "the task of distribution" became his chief occupation and he adopted the foundation as the best solution of the problems of stewardship as he saw them, Andrew Carnegie's influence was undoubtedly a predominant factor. It was certainly potent in the establishment and organization of the Rockefeller group of foundations. After his initial gifts to the University of Chicago, but several years before the endowment of the first of the great Rockefeller trusts, the elder Mr. Rockefeller had written to Mr. Carnegie in appreciation of what the latter had already done, approving his published statements, and indicating his hope that men of wealth would more and more come to follow his example. Later on the younger Mr. Rockefeller was a constant visitor to the library at the Carnegie home in New York, and in due season Mr.

Carnegie became an active trustee of the General Education Board.

This Board was the result of three converging influences: Mr. Rockefeller's own generously manifested interest in the program of the American Baptist Educational Society; the activities of the Peabody Education and the Slater Funds, of which Dr. Wickliffe Rose and Dr. Wallace Buttrick, each of them later to be President of the General Education Board, respectively were officers; and finally the Southern Education Board with the opportunities for constructive help in the Southern States demonstrated by it under the leadership of Mr. Robert C. Ogden. The Rockefeller Foundation, to which I shall refer again and again, was incorporated in 1913, and the Laura Spelman Rockefeller Memorial in 1920.

Fine leadership was soon developed in the boards brought into being through the endowments of Mr. Rockefeller and Mr. Carnegie, notably by Walter Hines Page, President Eliot of Harvard, Dr. Welch of Johns Hopkins, Elihu Root, President Butler, and last but not least President Alderman, all of them outstanding figures in that group which each generation produces for the guidance of the rest of us, and all of them exercising their personal influence upon the development of American foundations, entirely apart from their official relationship to any single trust.

Though some foundations have been created through the wills of men who had been practically unknown as philanthropists, this is not so in most of the important cases. Mr. Carnegie's corporation was in effect the funding of programs which he had already launched, and one has to look back to the record to see which of eight thousand organs or three thousand libraries were provided out of his own pocket or from the income of the trust he created in 1911. Similarly the Rosenwald Fund follows logically the generous personal gifts of Julius Rosenwald.

I should like at this point to say a word about one element in the picture not usually remembered, namely, the family of the donor. In the majority of cases, the establishment of a foundation must have been based on the expressed approval of the project by the members of the family, who would otherwise inherit the sum so donated. The important privilege which these members give up, as I see it, is not the possibility of added luxuries, but the freedom to carry out their own ideas in philanthropy, and I need not enlarge upon the satisfaction of having one's own way. At any rate, they certainly deserve more credit than they usually receive.

The donor is, of course, a man with a personality, and this personality must be reckoned with. Sometimes he tries to carry over too completely into his trust the policies he has found to work successfully in a business career. He has sometimes in his mind a beautiful picture of what he would like to accomplish, and proceeds to paint this picture in too great detail upon his deed of gift. He does not foresee the inevitable division of responsibility between the dead hand, which will soon be all that remains of him, and the living minds of trustees to come. It is unnecessary, as it would be ungracious, to cite examples of men who had the brains to make great fortunes, but who proved incompetent to distribute them wisely.

When the donor is alive and a member of the board he has created, he sometimes takes too active an interest in the proceedings, though, on the other hand, there are cases where he is scrupulous to the point of not being active enough. In general, the broader the discretion given by the donor to his trustees, the more useful to the community will his beneficence prove to be. This is even more true in the United States than it would be in England, because the public authorities here are far less willing to exercise freedom in authorizing desirable changes in the administration of a trust, though even in England the great Lord Eldon refused to permit an endowed school in Leeds to teach French and German, because these languages were not offered in the grammar school of the sixteenth century. Lest you may think that my fears are fanciful, let me give a few examples of actual foundations from the collection gathered by my friend, Ralph Hayes, of the New York Community Trust. There is the nineteenth-century endowment of an English pulpit which depended on the preacher's wearing a gown of a specified cut. We would not do that in the twentieth century, but we have our own examples ranging from an endowment for the permanent illumination

Past and Present

of a wife's tombstone, to a great trust for the centralized custodial care of orphans in a certain county in a certain state. The latter was made in spite of the fact that the whole trend of modern social theory is toward the placing of orphans in separate homes. Even if this were not so, there are not nearly orphans enough in the county in question and I understand that to carry out the trust, orphans have now to be imported from other regions.

Sometimes the original proposal is reasonable enough, but an unforeseen increase in the amount of the endowment emphasizes the need for freedom. A library was established in a church tower to be maintained by the dividends on certain shares of stock. These went up immensely in value, but the church can buy no books that won't fit into the tower, long since overcrowded. The entire value of the original estate with which the Sailor's Snug Harbor is endowed was $25,000. Its *income* is today more than $1,000,000, and the available supply of seafaring men is ever decreasing.

Uniform trusts for public uses are becoming generally known and will cut out some of these eccentric cases. Philanthropy, in the words of Mr. Hayes, is becoming more nearly foolproof, but the typical donor, the man capable of making a fortune and of giving it away, always has been, and, I think, always will be an individualist who will be inclined to do things in his own way.

At first the effect upon public opinion of the creation of the several Rockefeller and Carnegie foundations was very slight, largely because the public had become used to hearing continually of individual gifts from the two philanthropists and the change from their personal bounty to the grants of a chartered, tax-exempt institution seemed to make no particular difference. Probably this indifference would have continued if these foundations had limited their activities to library buildings, farm demonstrations and scientific research, though even in this last field you may recall the ugly picture of a scientific foundation which Sinclair Lewis introduced in *Arrowsmith*.

So soon, however, as the foundations became associated in the public mind with education in general and particularly with the social studies, suspicion was aroused in certain quarters, and charges of various kinds were made. This hostile attitude culminated in the Report of the Congressional Commission on Industrial Relations, transmitted in 1915. The report of the Director charges that the powers of the small group which controlled the "interests" was then being extended through the creation of "enormous privately managed funds for indefinite purposes," by the endowment of colleges and universities and the creation of funds for the pensioning of teachers; that two foundation groups, the Rockefeller and Carnegie, yielded an income twice as great as the appropriations of the Federal Government for education and social service; that the funds, though exempt from taxation, were subject to the dictates of the donors during their lives; that their policies must inevitably be colored, if not controlled, to conform to the policies of the corporations in which their funds were largely invested. These funds represent largely the result either of exploitation of American workers through low wages, or of the American public through high prices. They are subject to no public control. Their entrance into the field of industrial relations constitutes a menace to the national wealth.

The report deals also with the benumbing effect which it was asserted foundation gifts have upon funds from private citizens and public bodies. It was suggested to the Commission by its Director that Congress should require a Federal charter for all funds exceeding one million dollars, which should contain provision for the limitation of funds, both as to size and as to possibility of accumulation, specifications of the powers and functions, rigid inspection of finances, complete publicity, limiting of program to activities specifically mentioned in the articles of incorporation, and Congressional investigation of all endowed institutions, and finally that "as the only effective means of counteracting the influence of the foundations, as long as they are permitted to exist, consists in the activities of governmental agencies along similar lines, the appropriations of the Federal Government for education and social service should be correspondingly increased."

No Congressional action with reference to foundations followed the presentation of the Report, and there was little further public dis-

Past and Present 29

cussion in the years which followed. That the attitude of suspicion still persisted in some places was, however, evidenced by the fact that in 1925 the Regents of the University of Wisconsin adopted a resolution forbidding for the future the receipt of gifts from foundations. I may add that this action has been rescinded since the beginning of the present year.

From time to time one gets evidence of another type of criticism based on intellectual rather than social grounds. It is not unlike the attitude adopted by certain university professors toward their colleagues whose functions are administrative rather than scholarly. "The whole structure (of foundations) was designed for the benefit of scholarship and the conquest of wisdom. But our age and our national talent is one of organization. We are a mass-produced, newspapered, broadcasted and prohibited generation. The administrative camel has crowded the intellectual pilgrim out of his tent."

The manifestations of this attitude are often captious and to my mind unreasonable. Sometimes they take the form of denying to a foundation executive the right to hold even a layman's opinion on any debatable question. Nevertheless it is most important that such critics should not be discouraged in any way. Once in so often they save the foundation or one of its officers from tipping the scales in a matter of scholarly discussion by wielding, albeit unconsciously, the power of the purse.

Beside these general criticisms of the foundation as an institution, there have been, as is only natural, attacks upon individual trusts from time to time, as, for example, upon the Carnegie Foundation for its administration of the fund for professors' pensions, or upon a Rockefeller board for its alleged support of the Gary plan in the New York City schools. On the whole, however, such criticisms are few, but the degree to which this is due to the presence of wisdom on the part of the foundation on the one hand, or to the absence of knowledge and interest on the part of the public on the other, is a matter which I shall not attempt to discuss.

FOUNDATION POLICIES

FOUNDATION POLICIES

How far are we justified in speaking of foundation policies at all? Answering for myself, it depends a good deal on one's state of mind at the moment. Sometimes I find it hard to justify many of the grants made by the foundation for which I am in part responsible or any of the others, as finding their place in any reasoned program. At other times, I am very hopeful that our activities are measurably moving toward a more logical basis. Fewer gifts can be explained solely by corporate inability to say No, and more and more can find their place in an ordered pattern. Perhaps the safest answer is to say, as might be said of the university, that our policies are taking form but are as yet far from clear-cut.

Considering the sums involved and the significance of their wise use, one finds surprisingly little doctrinal writing as to foundation policies. The most interesting I know of is contained in the two annual printed reports of my predecessor, Dr. H. S. Pritchett, who wrote in 1922 on *A Science of Giving,* and in 1923 on the *Use and Abuse of Endowments.* It was in the former that he used a phrase which attracted at the time much public comment and some merriment, namely, "somebody must sweat blood with gift money if its effect is not to do more harm than good."

Offhand it seems absurd to think of the giving away of money as a difficult and possibly a dangerous process, but it was not long before not merely hostile critics but those who had every reason to be friendly recognized the truly difficult task of properly distributing large funds.

Please don't look for logical sequence in the discussion of foundation policies upon which I am about to embark. It isn't there. I've tried the different sections in half a dozen different orders without success. With so many different questions of principle arising in connection with the making of any particular grant, and so much to be said on both sides, I am consoling myself with the thought that perhaps the best way for you to grasp the many difficulties of the situation is precisely through the feeling of complexity and confusion which I am sure my treatment of the matter will furnish.

Let us turn first to finances, which is relatively the simplest part of the subject. As to the care of their capital funds, none of the American foundations suffered as did their predecessors in England from neglect or worse. In general, the trustees themselves take direct initiative as to investment policies. In the larger foundations, there is an investment officer working under the direction of a Chairman of the Finance Committee, chosen from the men of affairs making up the Board. The staff on the other hand is usually responsible for making up the operating budget. In trusts which are permanent in character, a reserve fund is customarily built up against impairment of principal.

In general, trustees are more interested in the soundness of the investments than in the amount of yield. Through the retirement of the steel bonds in which Mr. Carnegie's original gift was made, the Carnegie Corporation has recently had the responsibility of reinvesting the greater part of its capital, and a summary of its present investments may be of interest. One hundred and seventeen million dollars are in bonds, about half being in rails, and of the remainder, twenty-five million in public utilities, thirteen in industrials, twelve in Canadian or foreign government bonds. Ten million are in preferred and guaranteed stocks, and eight in United States Government securities. The average interest yield is 4.70 per cent.

In one of his reports, Dr. Pritchett has pointed out that trustees cannot fulfill their trust by exercising merely the negative aspects of prudence. Even gilt-edge securities sometimes lose their aureate quality. In his judgment, the price both of security and of a fair income yield is a constant and vigilant watchfulness exercised by experts all over securities held.

As to the selection of investments apart from their financial soundness, two questions arise. It not infrequently happens that an individual whose only interest is that of an investor may, through purchasing the stock of a given company, inadvertently acquire a large, sometimes a controlling influence in its affairs, and, in the minds of the public, a corresponding responsibility for its policies. To what degree should a foundation recognize this possibility in selecting securities for investment?

It may happen that an organization doing important work in a field in which some foundation is interested can be more effectively helped through the purchase of securities than by a direct grant. Assuming such securities to offer a reasonably sound investment, should the foundation favor their purchase? The Russell Sage Foundation has on occasion done so, and one of the important new trusts is said to be looking forward to making such an interrelation between its general program and its investments a fundamental part of its policy. On the other hand, most of the older foundations have felt that the two should be kept apart. Our own corporation has recently made a grant from income for the creation of a special fund from which such securities may be purchased, upon the understanding that they be kept separate from its investment accounts.

Experience has taught one most useful financial lesson, namely, that while future income must to some degree be obligated in the setting up of long-term enterprises, it is fatally easy to go too far and, in effect, seriously to limit in future years that freedom of initiative which is the most precious possession of the foundation. The Carnegie Corporation is still suffering in this respect from over-generosity in the years immediately following the war.

Problems of financial policy are alike, whatever may be the purpose of the foundation. Problems of operating policy, on the other hand, are far from uniform when the foundations have one of the more general charters already quoted, and even where the objective is clearly stated and the field of action correspondingly narrow, there remains plenty of opportunity for difference of opinion as to how the objective should be reached. For example, the resources may be concentrated at a single point or within a single region, or they may be deliberately distributed, as, for example, in the Guggenheim grants in support of aviation.

It may be that a full generation must elapse before the policies of any modern American foundation may be profitably discussed, since, from the nature of the case, decisions must tend to reflect the wishes of the donor if still living, or during the years immediately following his death, the influence of his personality as his friends and trustees remember it.

Certainly it is exceedingly hard to think straight among the number of conflicting claims, and a foundation does not always succeed. I have looked over the long list of our own grants since the foundation of the Corporation, and it is perfectly evident that a considerable number have been made from the heart rather than the head. Perhaps, however, this is on the whole as it should be, since it would have been impossible to carry out the spirit of a man like Andrew Carnegie through too cold-blooded a policy. Silas Bent has said of philanthropy, "At best it is an art; whether it can become a science is in doubt."

I think nearly all donors in making their gifts are thinking primarily of individuals to whom they will bring opportunity, but the ways in which this individual is to be reached vary widely. When the personal side is dominant, we find activities reaching from the distribution of individual doles to the careful selection of fellows and scholars by competent committees.

The granting of fellowships is a natural and important element in foundation policy and will be dealt with more fully later on. Individuals may be reached, however, not only through direct attack, but indirectly and by different paths, as, for example, through the individual's university or the learned society of which he is a member. Few foundations which publish their grants have the courage to help a man or a cause via an institution of uncertain financial or academic solidity. One of our unanswered questions is as to the number of really gifted people who do not fit into any scheme which would bring them to the favorable attention of existing foundations. Some generous person willing to take a chance might create a foundation to look after just such cases.

No foundation of which I have knowledge is particularly noted for consistency, but as one studies their works, certain general tendencies do seem to be discernible. Perhaps the most fundamental is the acceptance of responsibility

Foundation Policies 41

for initiative on the part of the trustees. The boards that deal only with applications received are becoming fewer and fewer. This initiative is usually expressed in what may be called "backing an idea." The idea sometimes grows out of the constructive policies of the foundation itself; sometimes it comes as a suggestion from the outside; most often I should say it is the outgrowth of informal discussion between those inside and those outside the foundation organization.

The years following the war witnessed a multitude of campaigns for the general endowment of colleges and universities, usually conducted by outside specialists. To these, the foundations were for years the most reliable contributors. The pressure still persists, applied often with great skill and intensity, but the recent tendency, I think, is to resist it unless the foundation can find within the limits of the objective set by the institution some piece of work which it would be glad to support on its merits and as a part of its own program. As an example, a grant for the training of museum curators as a part of the Harvard campaign of 1924 proved acceptable to that University, and as experience has shown, has proved of particular usefulness in developing our own interests in the fine arts and in the educational service of museums. In the Carnegie Corporation between 1921 and 1924, the number of grants made as contributions to campaigns for general endowment or equipment of institutions or annual support of operating organizations fell from 67% to 42% and in amount from 77% to 33% of the total. Although gifts for general purposes seem to be growing less attractive to the larger foundations, they are in general more welcome to the institutions concerned than any other form of help and in some cases at least they are most useful. Here, as elsewhere, a foundation must be on its guard against becoming the victim of its own formula.

There is a natural tendency on the part of foundations to limit their grants to the safe and sane. We find, however, here and there examples of real courage, such as the decision of the Rockefeller Foundation to work with the League of Nations when the current of American political opinion, and, to a less extent, of public opinion was running strongly in the other direction. The reports as to medical education, originally from the Carnegie Foundation and later from the General Education Board, furnish another case in point.

Some foundations apparently prefer to take the entire responsibility—and perhaps the glory—for any line of activity, whereas others seem to prefer to share both, particularly in enterprises involving possible social criticism. In some cases, they insist on participation by other foundations, in others by government agencies. Certain general questions of policy have to do with foundation aid *versus* or *plus* support from public funds. To quote Dr. Beardsley Ruml, of the Spelman Fund, "Public support is coercive on a minority. It should be used only for such objects as can clearly be shown to represent public responsibility, or general public benefit. For such objects, public support probably distributes the burden more equitably. . . . In general, private funds are most appropriately used for work of a novel or experimental character, or for activities which are not generally accepted as a public responsibility." When, however, the public responsibility becomes recognized, private agencies "may properly be expected to show good cause why all or part of their program should not be so transferred." He also points out that even when this stage is reached, it is useful, for a time at least, to have a certain amount of "privately supported work of similar character as an aid in maintaining high quality and efficiency of operation in public work." The outstanding example is to be found in the health activities of the Rockefeller Foundation, always undertaken in cooperation with public authorities, and always so directed as to transfer gradually the full costs of maintaining sound health standards to public taxation.

Some foundations obey almost literally the Scriptural injunction to sow beside all waters. Generally speaking, however, foundations strive toward unity, either in some single field or in a limited number of separate fields. This enables them to judge more intelligently among competing demands and gives hope of cumulative results. One way to bring about this unity is to ignore small enterprises and concentrate one's resources on a few striking gifts. These have always been more attractive to trustees, and apparently to the public also, than a large number of small ones. It must not be forgotten, however, that unity must sometimes be achieved, if at all, by a wisely selected pattern of small grants, rather than by a few strikingly large ones. Where or how, for example, would a single million dollar gift advance the cause of adult education today?

Policies as to the actual programs of any foundation fall naturally into certain classes. There are such positive decisions, for example, as that by which the Trustees of the Murry and Leonie Guggenheim Foundation concentrated the funds at their disposal upon dental clinics, or equally clear-cut negative decisions, as when the Carnegie Corporation decided to build no more public libraries. This situation deserves a word of comment. Here was an activity with which the donor's name had been more closely connected than any other one which had been carried on for many years and with uniform public approval; but assuming the donor's purpose to have been to set an example which communities might be persuaded to follow, his trustees had to determine whether the time had come when further gifts would hinder rather than help in carrying out that purpose. The decision did not involve leaving the library field, to which as much money is being devoted since the decision as before, but it is now for library service rather than library construction.

More often questions of policy emerge rather more gradually, and it is only as one looks backward that they are discernible. Take, for instance, the question of the direction of opinion. Propaganda was, of course, of the essence of the religious foundation which preceded the modern type, and twenty years ago, if any board were unanimous in regarding as socially desirable the spread of a given opinion, there was no hesitation in taking action in supporting this spread. The reports of early years are full of examples, but as one follows the record through succeeding years, it is evident that the realization is coming that while deliberate propagation of opinion is a perfectly legitimate function for the individual, it is not the wisest way to use funds that are tax-exempt and therefore "affected with a public interest." This is entirely apart from the question whether, in any given case, those in charge of such funds may, as individuals, be sincerely in favor of the spread of the idea in question. Or, to put it in another way, the discovery and distribution of facts from which men and women may draw their own conclusions offers the foundation a field sufficiently wide and sufficiently vital to the welfare of humanity.

It is, of course, much easier to announce principles of this kind than to apply them in actual cases. Here is an instance where common sense would prove a better guide than principle. Whatever we may find out about cancer, there is no question that early recognition is of the very first importance, and this depends upon an early examination, and early examination depends upon nothing more or less than an indoctrination of the public upon this particular point.

One of the most difficult problems has to do with the degree to which a foundation should combine with its function of giving money that of giving advice or even of giving orders. This touches alike its treatment of enterprises it helps with money and those for which aid is refused. Of course there is no easy answer. The foundation executive is frequently the best qualified to give sound counsel or even to assume control, and the human temptation to do both is ever present. On the other hand, in his particular case the power he wields is only secondarily that of his own wisdom. Certainly the bulk of recent criticism of foundation policies has been directed against what the writers believe to be the dangers attending the exercise of such power.

As to relations with other agencies, though here again there is no clear-cut line to be discerned, foundations either tend toward freedom from entangling alliances, or towards a willingness to accept very close relations with institutions or organizations, such relations, for example, as the Carnegie Corporation has maintained since its organization with the American Library Association, or the Laura Spelman Memorial with the National Council of Parent Education. On the other hand, the Commonwealth Fund reports that, as a matter of policy, it "devotes the greater part of its resources to projects for which it assumes administrative or advisory responsibility."

Certain foundations evidently try to limit

their activities to fields where the objectives are clear-cut and where results can be measured. The contrasting tendency may, I think, be exemplified in our own field of operations. At any rate, one of my colleagues bewails my own tendency to recommend grants which, in his judgment, dissipate the energies of the Carnegie Corporation in vague support of vague social or educational objectives. Out of our friendly debates on the subject, I think I recognize another general question of foundation policy. Concretely, is a foundation justified in interesting itself in adult education or in the fine arts? That we have wasted some money in both, there is no possible question. That in the aggregate our contribution to the richness of human life has been substantial and has in it the elements of permanency, I hope the future will demonstrate.

It is hard to remember that the chief justification of a foundation grant lies frequently not in the help it may give to the institution receiving it, nor even the quality of the work itself, but in its significance as a demonstration. For example, a grant of art material to a typical girls' college would undoubtedly be better used than if it were made to a boys' college, but if given to the latter, it would set an example where examples are more needed. Too many people assume unconsciously today that interest in the fine arts is what the biologists call a sex-limited character.

Or again, in choosing agencies to be helped, at least indirectly, by selection as the locus for an experiment or demonstration, shall we take the poor and needy, which is the natural temptation, or, more prudently, if we think in terms of the value of our investment, shall we apply the rule that unto him that hath shall be given? In these matters one must consider not merely the foundation itself and its place at the bar of public opinion, but also the effect on those who either make application for help or may reasonably expect help to be offered. Foundation decisions seem to be serving more and more as a measuring rod of merit, to a degree alarming to those who are familiar with their very human limitations. Either affirmative or negative action by a foundation may have an influence upon other possible contributors much more powerful than it should.

Foundation Policies 51

Care in selection is, of course, important, and haste doesn't usually work for wisdom, but we must remember that while the donor is delaying, the recipient may be losing that initial capacity for enthusiasm which may well be the decisive factor of success in any proposed undertaking.

This variety of policy is to be found not only in the choice of grants and the selection of beneficiaries, but in the conditions under which they are given.

The sharpest line that can be drawn is between the gift entirely without conditions and that dependent upon action by others, usually the raising of an equivalent sum from other sources. The General Education Board has pointed out somewhere that conditional gifts of eighty million dollars made by it to colleges, universities and medical schools have been the cause of contributions of twice that sum from other sources. The conditional gift was at first by far the most popular type of foundation grant, and is still widely used, but, as I have said elsewhere, it may be questioned whether in some instances a conditional offer does not put too powerful a weapon in the hands of persons perhaps not fully qualified to exercise the responsibility of using it. It would not be difficult to cite instances in which local communities, or alumni, or religious bodies, have been dragooned by the use of this weapon into making contributions beyond their means and beyond the real needs of the institution in question. You may remember the judgment of the French cynic that more harm is done in the world by the righteous than the unrighteous, because the former are never restrained by the dictates of conscience. Certainly so far as our own institution is concerned, there is a measurable drop in the number of appropriations made with accompanying conditions. As I pointed out to our trustees two years ago, while 33% of all grants made up to that time were voted with conditions, in the last three years only 11% were conditioned in any respect, and only 2% were contingent on the securing of funds from other sources.

While, as I have said, most foundation grants go to colleges, universities, museums and other institutions of a permanent character, there is constant opportunity, to put it mildly, for them to contribute to the needs of associations of different kinds, and certain important policies have to do with their relations to such organizations. Most of the professional and scholarly groups of this character, such as the American Library Association or the Modern Language Association, were formed before the war, but the majority of the organizations for social purposes grew out of war activities, and it is no easy task for a foundation to determine in any individual case whether the agency fulfills a continuing need or is merely the outcome of a very human desire on the part of individuals to ensure the continuation of agreeable and reasonably remunerative careers initiated under war or post-war conditions.

After the decision as to which, if any, of these organizations should receive help toward its overhead expenses as part of the general program of a foundation, questions arise as to the form in which this help should be given. In general, foundations are shifting from annual grants of an indefinite tenure to grants for a specified time, and are tending, though not so uniformly, toward grants progressively decreasing in amount, on the assumption that this will force the agency to establish other sources of income, so that when foundation help comes to an end, its work may go on.

All such bodies are eager, and naturally eager, to receive gifts for endowment. The foundations reply that they limit their endowment grants to institutions having, humanly speaking, the certainty of permanence. This, however, does not dispose of the argument—it merely shifts it. Take the case of a leader of high ideals and undoubted ability, who naturally desires to make permanent the work he has organized and is carrying on so successfully. The foundation is inclined to think the results are due primarily to his own personality, and would in large measure cease at his death or retirement. The leader is quite sure he has devised a system which will run forever. In some cases a compromise has been effected through bringing such organizations under the aegis of some university.

The separate institutes of which I spoke a little earlier are also eager for endowment, and much the same question of policy arises in their case. Such an institution cannot be dismissed as a one-man show, but it does lack the possibilities of criticism which a university—I won't say enjoys, but possesses. One independent organization, the Marine Biological Laboratory at Woods Hole, has, in its deed of trust, deliberately provided for recurrent criticism of its affairs by a permanent committee of review, made up of representatives of three great national scientific organizations, and biologists selected by their colleagues in six designated universities. Every ten years, this committee must review the work of the Laboratory, and it has the power to initiate steps toward the modification or the termination of the work. This device, already adopted elsewhere, gives hope to those who believe that the difficulties attending the control of a national institute by a single university outweigh the advantages to be gained.

Gifts for buildings occupy a half-way place between temporary grants and permanent endowment. A building may be most useful to the institution concerned and a suitable and handsome memorial to the donor, whether his name be used or not. On the other hand, it is, I think, generally assumed that this very attractiveness makes it easier for an institution to secure a building from other than foundation sources. Early foundation grants were largely in the form of buildings, then there was a distinct drop, and I think recently a tendency toward an increase in the number of such gifts. The later grants, however, can usually be recognized as cases in which the building may be regarded as a form of equipment essential to the carrying out of an idea.

About one policy, there seems to me there can be no difference of opinion among intelligent people, that of the fullest publicity—and I draw a distinction between publicity and advertising—as to finances and activities. While such information is scrupulously furnished in the case of the foundations I have mentioned, the majority of the smaller trusts fail to do so, and I myself, who am professionally interested in such matters and ought to be in a position to secure available information, have been able to obtain nothing whatever regarding three foundations, the announced capitalization of which aggregates seventy-five million dollars. And yet all these are public institutions, at least

Foundation Policies

to the degree of being relieved from taxation. In my judgment, public confidence in foundations in general may depend to a greater degree than is at present realized upon public knowledge of their operations.

It would be most desirable for the newer foundations at least to establish contact with the older ones, but it seems to be the rare exception for them to do so. In my own experience of more than seven years, only three foundations of any importance have shown any inclination to ask advice and to profit by the experience of their elders, and one of these was within the past month. If a new foundation were to seek and obtain the help which would gladly be furnished, the experience of twenty-five years would be immediately applicable as to the formulation of general policies, the sifting of proposals and applications upon the basis of competent and disinterested advice, the setting up and budgeting of specific projects, and perhaps most of all, the selection of personnel. Apparently the idea prevails that once the money is provided, the rest will be easy.

We have clearly before us a situation in which you are not going to hear from me, or from any one else—"the conclusion of the whole matter," but I hope I have given you some idea of the difficulties which daily face the philanthropoid, to use the pet name applied to those who give away the money of others. I hope also you will agree with me as to the desirability that a foundation should seek to steer a middle course, avoiding on the one side the rigidity and sometimes the autocracy which result from too narrowly defined a policy, and, on the other, the danger of scattering its resources over "the dry sands of humanity's constant need, without any permanent result in the progress of mankind."

ORGANIZATION AND PROCEDURE

ORGANIZATION AND PROCEDURE

Having said something as to how the modern American foundation has come into existence and something of its policies, let us see how it actually operates. These millions of dollars which are distributed annually do not give themselves away. In every case under discussion, whether a grant be made or not, something has happened, some decision has been reached. The factors in this decision are, on the one side, the trustees of the foundation, its permanent staff, the men and women called into temporary service, and voluntary advisers of different types—sometimes special commissions are created to deal with important questions. On the other side is the potential recipient of the grant in question, usually but not always a chartered institution.

As I have already indicated, grants may be either constructive, as fitting into a program previously decided upon by the foundation, or they may be defensive, as representing the immediate needs, or at any rate, the desires of an applicant. In the latter case, the active proponent, sometimes an organization officer, sometimes a professional fund-raiser, sometimes a free lance, is always an interesting figure. He is convinced not only of the righteousness but of the immediacy of his cause and its proper place at the head of the priority list. He cannot understand why there should be any doubt in the minds of others, and yet in the great majority of cases he must inevitably fail of his quest. In a typical year, the Rockefeller Foundation, for example, found itself unable to grant six hundred and twenty-two applications. These included twenty-nine in public health, one hundred and forty-eight in medical education, fifty-two in general education, one hundred and twenty for local institutions, and one hundred and ninety-four for personal aid. The remaining seventy-nine were of a miscellaneous character. At about the same time, the Carnegie Corporation received three hundred and ninety-seven applications, totaling more than forty million dollars, of which but sixty-two could be granted, thirty-three of them being renewals.

Organization and Procedure 63

Broadly speaking, foundations may be divided into those with a tight and those with a loose type of operation. The former tend to insist on formal applications, even when the original suggestion comes from themselves. They require that institutions to be helped should conform to certain standards. They are most unlikely to make a grant out of line with their established and announced policies. The looser type does not insist on these formalities. One foundation discourages applications on the ground that the boot should be on the other foot, and the technical request should come, of course after the fullest possible exchange of information, from those charged with the distribution of the fund. These latter feel that the objective is to get at the individual who is capable of doing something worth while, rather than to carry out a predetermined procedure. Andrew Carnegie used to put it bluntly: "Find the efficient man and enable him to do his work."

While the foundations of this second type are not less mindful of their responsibilities and are, let us hope, equally careful in budgetary and other similar matters, their actual programs are harder to defend on the ground of uniformity. Realizing the ever present danger of dissipating their funds, one of the larger foundations of this type sets aside in its budget a definite figure, and the grants which do not fit into its regular program are limited to the amount of this appropriation.

The foundations find the same difficulty which the universities have found in the selection of trustees. The type of person wanted is already very busy; sometimes the very man who would hesitate to become the executor of an estate without planning to devote a substantial share of his time to the responsibilities involved, will not hesitate to accept a place on a foundation board without really thinking through the obligations he is assuming. In general, however, the foundations have been fortunate in finding trustees who have given freely and helpfully, not only of their "sound judgment, wide experience and imaginative discrimination," but of their time as well. Of course when a foundation is limited to a single field, as the Juilliard Musical Foundation, some special competence in that

Organization and Procedure

field is desirable, but not at the expense of the more general qualifications. Sometimes, as in the case of colleges, a trustee's devotion carries him a little too far, but as time goes on, all are beginning to understand more clearly the distinction between the responsibility of the staff for details of administration and of the trustees for general direction of policy. One president believes that the best the officers can expect from the trustees is "the inspiration of their association and their discerning judgment upon the proposals that may be made."

In looking over the list of the trustees of the important funds, one cannot fail to be impressed by the number of really distinguished citizens who are evidently glad to accept membership. Membership, however, is almost wholly limited to men, revealing once more the lag between what we all know today as to the capacity of women in positions of responsibility and our willingness to apply that knowledge. Only two boards have faced the problems which the passing of the years brings to any self-perpetuating body, the Rockefeller Foundation and the General Education Board having recently adopted the drastic policy of retiring trustees and officers alike at the age of sixty-five.

Before I leave the question of the trustee, I ought to add that there are certain foundations, some of them with capital funds running well into the millions, which enjoy full exemption from taxation, but for which the donor, either through ignorance or design, has set up a board of lay figures, wholly under his own control. This situation has elements of real danger, not only to the organizations concerned, but to all foundations, and it is to be hoped that a better understanding of the obligations as well as the privileges of funding one's fortune, aided perhaps by the pressure of a more fully informed public opinion, will bring about a change for the better.

The permanent staff is the next element in the picture to consider. In general, the administrative overhead for a foundation is relatively low, but should not be so low as to prevent competent administrative direction. Most of the staff members, as I have said, come from universities and have usually been university officers.

Organization and Procedure 67

What shall I say about the chief executive officer of a foundation? There are obvious elements of embarrassment in my saying anything at all, but these must be faced. He is usually, but not always, a trustee. I don't think this makes much difference, for his peculiar responsibility and, to be frank, his power, lie in the selection of material to lay before his board, not in his individual vote. Let us assume that he possesses in reasonable degree the qualities required for any responsible administrative position, honesty, executive capacity, fair-mindedness, intelligence. What does he need in addition for this particular job? Well, he needs patience and good humor. No matter how trivial any proposal may seem to another, it is never trivial to the person making it. He must be immune to cajolery, for it is a sad fact that many of the people with whom he has to do are convinced that the righteousness of their cause justifies any means short of murder to advance it. He must be what is called a "good waiter." He must practice what President Butler calls the art of being well-informed, and must see that his colleagues practice it. This applies concretely to the specific proposals presented, where often the best that can be hoped from the proponent is certain selected aspects of the truth. More significantly it applies to general information regarding the fields in which his foundation is working. Nor is this all; he must be ready to recognize new opportunities when the ever-shifting scene of modern life makes a change in policy desirable. This means for himself and his colleagues much reading of reports, a watchful eye for the words of men with creative minds, the assurance of personal contact with the people that count, and the seeing of things worth seeing. And he must accomplish and direct all this without so complicating his existence that he loses the power to see the forest rather than the trees. It is rather a large order and one that is not likely to be filled to every one's complete satisfaction this side of the millennium.

To ensure competent conduct of its affairs, a foundation must be adequately staffed, for correspondence, accountancy, editorial, and other services, but in these it does not differ from any similar organization. There is, however, one function which it alone can perform and which thus far it has neglected. Once a grant has been made, it tends to be forgotten, the organization becomes absorbed in new projects, and fails to conduct that running audit of its experiences which would prove most valuable, both as a historic record and as a guide to its own future policy. This opportunity is, however, becoming recognized, and foundations are selecting staff members competent to conduct this audit without interfering with the affairs of the recipients of grants.

In practically every field with which a foundation may be concerned, there is a need for advice of professional competence, whether such advice is to be found in the permanent staff or is obtained *ad hoc* as needed. Which it shall be depends in part on what might be called the general traditions of the foundation in question. Mr. Carnegie's trusts with their relatively limited personnel reflect his own business habits, just as the elder Mr. Rockefeller's desire not to assume responsibility beyond the establishment and organization of his funds, has emphasized the place of professional advisers in the foundations he created. It depends in part on whether the foundation itself undertakes the direction of operations. Or perhaps it is the other way round. When you have a professional staff, you are likely to find yourself running a business.

The practice is growing of substituting for permanent staff experts temporary officers, nearly always university professors on leave of absence. This gives to the foundation a wider range of selection and leaves it free to change the technical character of its interest without turning off an officer who might have difficulty in finding another position.

The degree to which voluntary help from persons wholly outside the staff is sought and rendered is not generally realized. From one of our recent annual reports, that for 1925, I have checked up the number of such individuals whose advice regarding the program for that year was sought by the Corporation. There were two hundred and eighty-seven in all, eighty-one in adult education, sixty in the arts, twenty-six in library matters, thirty-eight in connection with a modern language study, and twenty-four for other questions.

More and more the help which foundations are receiving from outside sources comes not

Organization and Procedure 71

from individuals, but from groups, usually committees of national professional or scholarly bodies, or councils made up from such organizations. When, as sometimes happens, no such organized body is available, it has been our experience that the most distinguished experts in any field are glad to give their best service as members of informal advisory committees. Such help is always freely offered, and on their part, the foundations welcome not only advice concerning applications, but also suggestions and recommendations as to other related activities. Indeed, it is my expectation that in time, the latter will outnumber the former.

Sometimes a non-operating foundation will turn to an operating one for help. The Carnegie Corporation is, naturally, likely to refer its programs as to educational studies to the Foundation next door and those in experimental science to the Institution at Washington, but we sometimes go outside of our family group. Mr. Carnegie was interested in music, but the Corporation which bears his name and which wishes to reflect in its program this interest of the donor, has but little competence in the field. It is an open secret that the help of the Juilliard Foundation is called upon in the distribution of our funds for music.

I have gone into these matters in considerable detail because there is one underlying question upon which it is important for us to see clearly. The legal and moral responsibility for carrying out the provisions of any of these trusts lies not upon its officers but upon its board of trustees. Now these trustees may be most devoted and most punctilious in carrying out their responsibilities, but it is literally impossible for them to examine personally the hundreds of cases on which they must act, either positively or negatively. In a well-ordered foundation all applications are reported, and action favorable or otherwise, recorded in the minutes; but when the chief executive officer, with or without the help of associates or advisers, selects certain proposals for favorable consideration, he actually exercises the power of final and negative decision in the case of the others, and necessarily these constitute the great majority. "Very few of these cases are outstanding, many are worthy, the great majority commonplace," but even in

Organization and Procedure 73

the case of the latter, they are commonplace only to the disinterested outsider, not to those who have faith in them. Trustees and executives alike are working to reduce to a minimum this element of personal decision. By deciding to refrain from certain fields, by budgeting and sub-budgeting, the trustees may automatically cut out certain cases. Some boards split up into sub-committees to give more intensive study to certain types of application. Another designates a member of the board to make a rapid review of all of the data in non-recommended cases.

The most important factor, however, is the increasing use of these intermediate advisory bodies, presumably competent not only to give counsel as to the worth-while character of specific proposals, but to study the relative merits of competing proposals and, in effect, to establish a sort of priority list for the guidance of foundations. While offering a valuable safeguard against the inadvertent neglect of an important application, these bodies are most useful in helping the foundation to build up what I have called its offensive program. The first two million dollars distributed by the Carnegie Corporation in 1911 and 1912 was all voted in direct response to applications. Of the two million voted in 1928, 68% involved consultation with some representative organization.

FOUNDATION ACTIVITIES

FOUNDATION ACTIVITIES

Thus far you have heard a good deal of the why and the how of foundations. It is none too soon to say something as to just what they do. Let us begin with one having a relatively small capitalization and a definite objective. Since its organization in 1925, the Guggenheim Memorial Fund has given opportunities for foreign travel and for creative work to two hundred and seventy-eight Americans, without regard to sex, race, creed or color. The Fund has developed a technique for the wise selection of individuals which is setting a high standard for us all to follow. An impressive list of the creative work resulting from this single benefaction could be made up, but I shall give only one example: *John Brown's Body* was written by a Guggenheim fellow during his incumbency. The recent announcement that the Fund is inaugurating a series of Mexican fellowships is welcome news.

Meanwhile, the Commonwealth Fund, as

part of its program, has brought one hundred and fifteen carefully selected university graduates from Great Britain and the Dominions to the United States.

Turning to a foundation whose charter is general, the Carnegie Corporation got under way in 1911. Since then it has appropriated, in round figures, from the income of its principal fund: to the Carnegie Institute of Pittsburgh, chiefly for the endowment of the Institute of Technology, twenty-six million dollars; for security in old age to professors, chiefly through the Carnegie Foundation, twenty-two million; colleges and universities, twenty-one million; public library buildings (discontinued after 1917), twelve million; research and publication, seven million; to the National Research Council and other learned societies and professional associations, fourteen million; Carnegie Institution of Washington, seven million; other purposes, eleven million.

From the income of a special fund of ten million dollars established by Mr. Carnegie for Canada and the British Colonies, about seven million dollars has been voted; more than four million for colleges and universities; more than

Foundation Activities 79

one million for public libraries; two million for miscellaneous purposes.

Since its establishment in 1918 by Mrs. Stephen V. Harkness, the Commonwealth Fund has distributed nearly fifteen million dollars from income, almost wholly in the fields of child welfare, health, and education. It is interesting to note that of this sum about two and one-half million were spent in Europe for the first two of these objectives in such a way as to furnish post-war relief of a constructive character. Over four million has gone to mental hygiene and child guidance, two and one-half million to a series of five-year programs in child health, including one in Austria, one and a quarter million in the interest of rural hospitals, and about the same for medical research and other health objectives. The Commonwealth Fund fellowships already referred to have cost another million.

The Laura Spelman Rockefeller Memorial was organized in 1919 and in 1929 merged with the Rockefeller Foundation. In the ten years of its activities, it made grants, in round figures, as follows, in addition to generous gifts to New York charities and to the

Y.M.C.A. and the Y.W.C.A.: Social Sciences twenty-two million dollars; Social Technology three million dollars; Child Welfare, primarily for child study and parental education, seven million dollars; Interracial three million dollars; Recreation two and a half million dollars; International five million dollars; unclassified six million dollars. In addition, special memorials were created before the merger, aggregating seventeen million dollars and including five million dollars for the Great Smoky Mountains project, and ten million dollars to establish the Spelman Fund of New York.

These furnish representative pictures of the general activities of foundations of different types. You may still want to know what they do in particular.

The technique of educational research has been immeasurably advanced in recent years, and several foundations have found ways to apply the new techniques. Sometimes they have done this in cooperation, as in the case of the voluminous study of Educational Finance. More frequently, one foundation undertakes the entire financial load; for example, in sub-

Foundation Activities

ject matter studies, the General Education Board supported a comprehensive study of the classics, the Carnegie Corporation those of the modern languages and the social studies. Another favorite form for foundation activity is the study of professional education in different fields. Inquiries which have literally revolutionized medical education began with that of the Carnegie Foundation in 1910, but have since then been conducted by the General Education Board. Initial studies in dental, legal and engineering education have all been made by the Carnegie Foundation, the last named having been followed by a study of the Society for the Promotion of Engineering Education, financed by the Carnegie Corporation. The Corporation has also financed a very thorough study of training for librarianship, and is now supporting studies in forestry and architecture.

These studies have proved to be very costly, and there has come to be a feeling that substantial economies in money, and probably in time as well, might be effected by the development of an intermediate step between the formulation of the project and the setting up of the machinery for carrying that project into effect. An analogous step is found in the development of important industrial projects. In the case of a scholarly undertaking, it has been tried out in a few instances by freeing two or three individuals selected for the direction of the study from other responsibilities and giving them an opportunity to prepare what might be termed the detailed working drawings of the project.

For a term of years, the Commonwealth Fund set aside a generous sum to be used in less comprehensive educational studies, from which much important material has resulted. Mental hygiene, having become a repository of new knowledge and a subject of active institutional and community interest, has offered opportunity to a number of foundations, notably the Laura Spelman Memorial and the Commonwealth.

There is one interesting example of cooperation involving a foundation, a state system of education, and a group of colleges, both tax supported and endowed, in the eight-year study of the relations between secondary and higher education in which the Carnegie Foundation, the Pennsylvania Department of Public Education, and the Pennsylvania colleges are now engaged. The General Education Board, the Rosenwald Fund, and the Carnegie Corporation are at present conducting a joint study of certain educational and library problems in the Southern States for the double purpose of avoiding duplication and of making sure that no essential element in the problems should be overlooked by all three.

Let me now turn to the largest single body of coordinated foundation activity. Following the demonstration by United States army officers in Cuba and Panama as to what competent public health administration can accomplish, the Rockefeller Foundation undertook a program of cooperation with governmental bodies throughout the world in this field, the results of which have now their permanent place in human history. Up to the end of 1929, this program has cost more than forty million dollars. The Rockefeller Foundation has also distributed nearly seventy millions for medical education, chiefly in foreign countries.

The sister foundation, the General Education Board, having selected medical education as a field of concentrated activity, set to work to strengthen existing leadership, as, for example, in its support of the Johns Hopkins Medical School, and, to a lesser degree, at Washington University, Vanderbilt University, and elsewhere. In some cases, it took the initiative in the creation of an entirely new school, as at Rochester. Since 1919, the General Education Board has spent nearly seventy-three and a half million dollars in this field. Meanwhile it has distributed almost eighty-three million dollars among universities and colleges in the United States, including nearly fourteen million to negro institutions.

Other foundations have also turned to demonstrations in public health. The Milbank Memorial, for example, has already contributed two and a quarter millions to a ten year demonstration of modern health service in three typical communities, a rural district, Cattaraugus County, N. Y., a medium-sized city, Syracuse, and a section of New York City, Yorkville.

In some cases, a foundation will feel its way by a series of exploratory operations before committing itself to a large scale program. In

Foundation Activities 85

June, 1924, the Carnegie Corporation called a small group together for advice regarding adult education. From that initial conference, there followed, first, the organization of four basic studies to bring together the facts; second, a series of other conferences, four of them regional and two of them nationwide in their scope; third, the organization of the American Association for Adult Education in 1926 and the assurance of support for its general expenses over a period of years by the Corporation; fourth, the setting aside in the annual budget of the Corporation of a certain sum for studies and demonstrations in adult education, to be allocated on the recommendation of the directors of the new association.

It often happens that some activity becomes so closely associated in the public mind with a given foundation, sometimes from the nature of its charter, sometimes from its deliberate choice of program, that the foundation in question, if for no other reason than to avoid criticism, is likely to support any worth-while activity in this field. Any library proposal, for example, is likely to come to the Carnegie Corporation; any suggestion in the field of social work to the

Russell Sage; in the cause of international peace to the Carnegie Endowment; in music to the Juilliard or the Presser.

Sometimes a foundation sees an opportunity to perform a useful local purpose and at the same time to advance a new profession. The action of the Russell Sage Foundation in contributing over a million dollars during seven years to the Regional Plan of New York has not only performed a service of fundamental importance to the community with which the foundation is largely concerned, but it has advanced the profession of city and regional planning in countless ways.

We have still to deal with the far more difficult question of the advancement of existing knowledge by the support of scientific research. It is, of course, impossible to draw a sharp line, because many of the activities which I have already described result either in creating favorable conditions for the general prosecution of research or themselves involve particular researches. One might perhaps make a distinction between the cases where new knowledge is a secondary result of foundation activity, and where it is the direct objective. The whole program of the Carnegie Institution of Washington, for example, is a research program, in which fundamental research is being carried forward in eleven different divisions.

Many of the largest grants from other foundations have definitely been in the interest of research. Until last year, the largest of these was the grant of five million dollars from the Carnegie Corporation in 1921 to provide the National Research Council with a building in Washington and an endowment, but this has now been surpassed by the decision of the International Education Board to contribute six million dollars for a single project, i.e., the erection and endowment of a two hundred inch reflecting telescope in Southern California.

The most brilliant success attending any single grant made by the Carnegie Corporation was undoubtedly the development of insulin by three Canadian men of science at the University of Toronto. It was a beautiful example of what is called cooperative research. This idea of men of different talents and skills and experiences working together for a common end is a fascinating one, and I confess that our trustees for a number of years deliberately sought opportunities to foster it in other fields, but thus far without success. Perhaps the following quotation may give the reason. It might be put more considerately for foundation feelings, but the writer has earned by his own record in research the right to speak his mind:

"Research councils and foundations organize cooperative researches, thinking that the shy truth can be snared by the noisy advance of a well-drilled company of technicians, forgetting that discovery was ever a solitary task, in which cooperation must be spontaneous, asked as the need arises by one lonely seeker from another."

On the other hand, there are many who approve the recent organization of research councils within universities, as providing a fairer distribution of money (most of it from foundation sources) and of time, through the relief of promising workers of other duties, than obtained under departmental control.

No adverse criticism has attended foundation contributions, which have been substantial, toward providing what might be called the fundamental tools for research, including revolving funds for publication to scholarly societies and the support of such series as the biological and social science abstracts.

One cannot discuss the relationship of the foundations to research without making clear the type of research we have in mind. The word has been notoriously abused. Every American city has its chamber of commerce, and that chamber has its research department, but their aggregate contributions aren't going to add greatly to the sum of human knowledge. There is, however, a very substantial body of useful and disinterested research, some of it fundamental in character, performed by commercial and industrial bodies, which in 1927 contributed two hundred millions of the total of two hundred and seventeen devoted to research in the United States. To the degree that industrial and commercial research and the corresponding activities of the Federal and State Governments meet the need for what might be called secondary research, the responsibilities of the foundations are correspondingly lightened. On the other hand, the prosecution of fundamental researches will remain one of the major opportunities, perhaps the major opportunity, of the foundations, so long as they themselves endure. For the layman, it is almost impossible to conceive either the imagination or the patience and persistence which fundamental research demands. Last month, some of you may have read of the creation of an oxygen atom at the University of Chicago. Did you notice that the first confirming photograph was made after ten thousand failures, and that for the second, the experimenter had to make twenty-four thousand more exposures? Or did you notice in the more recent report regarding the experiments in the velocity of light from the Mt. Wilson Observatory of the Carnegie Institution that thirty thousand separate measurements had been made before the results were announced to the public?

CONCLUSION

CONCLUSION

These lectures have turned out to be a good deal less informative and a good deal more advisory than I had intended, and it may be that they should be regarded as an attempt on my part to set up that body of foundation doctrine, the absence of which I have already deplored. For what it may be worth, therefore, let me in this closing chapter summarize the ideas which, if I had the chance, I should try to put into the minds of those concerned with the establishment of a new foundation.

Provided its funds and its policies are in the hands of disinterested and able people, a foundation of any size, of broad or of narrow purpose, has the possibilities of being useful. There is room for great variety, not only in policy, but in procedure. There is a place for the foundation with principal permanently set apart, and for the fund which distributes both capital and interest; for one which conducts its own operations, and one which limits its activities to the distribution of grants.

Donors, trustees, staff must all be on their guard against illusions of omniscience, or of omnipotence, or both. Broadly speaking, a foundation is likely to succeed in so far as all concerned approach their duties in the realization that the money which they distribute is not their own, and that, furthermore, the contribution of money is always secondary in importance to the work of men and women of creative minds and devoted lives. Every effort must be made to secure sound and disinterested advice, whether from the foundation staff or otherwise, and to provide for constant and searching criticism of operations. Provision must also be made for accurate and frequent public reports, both as a matter of moral obligation and of practical wisdom.

A foundation must be willing to take the initiative; it must show courage as well as prudence; it must realize that the value of individual enterprises can't always be measured by general formulas. A potential distributor of funds must be particularly careful as to how he gives advice to possible recipients thereof as to the conduct of their affairs. It must ever be on its guard against indulging in propaganda, even

Conclusion 95

such virtuous propaganda as I am at this moment engaged in.

As a social instrument the mobility of the foundation gives it certain very definite assets, of which it should take full advantage. Promptness of decision is one, and another is the power of continued action, if necessary over a period of years. It cannot retain its freedom of initiative if it piles up obligations against future income. It should similarly be on guard against dissipating its resources, either by making grants for trivial or unproductive purposes, or by contributing funds which it is reasonable to expect would otherwise be forthcoming from other sources.

The foundation should be alert to seek out and to enter new fields where help is needed, provided its resources are sufficient either to make a substantial immediate contribution, or to continue its help long enough to achieve a cumulative effect. Also, and this is, I think, harder, it should show decision in withdrawing before the day of diminishing returns has arrived and its activities have settled down to ruts and routine.

Year in and year out fundamental research

will probably offer to the foundation the most important but not the sole field of activity. Fact-finding and demonstration must not be overlooked, nor the publication and distribution of pertinent information.

So much for theory. Thus far I have been leaving out perhaps the most potent factor of all, the factor of human personality. Take, for example, the General Education Board in the days of its greatest activity. All the printed descriptions in the world would fail to set forth the peculiar qualities which each of its leading officers brought to the task, and the influence of these qualities upon its accomplishment—Mr. Sage, who has been described as a hard-boiled idealist; Dr. Buttrick, with his uncanny art of effacing his own personality, while getting his own way (and usually a very wise way); Abraham Flexner's far-ranging mind, his detective's capacity for pouncing upon the significant detail, and, I hope he will forgive my adding, his rare powers of dramatization.

The Carnegie Institution of Washington was a great institution under Dr. Woodward, and has remained a great institution under his successor, Dr. Merriam, but the two administrations when compared reflect clearly, and, I think, quite legitimately, the different personalities of the two presidents. Similarly, the many-sided interests and capacities of President Butler are setting their stamp upon the activities of the Carnegie Endowment. It is seldom that an organization finds a leader with the courage of Dr. Pritchett, who is now retiring after twenty-four years of service as President of the Carnegie Foundation. Like any human enterprise, the Foundation during these years has made its mistakes, but they have never been those of timidity.

Even if we knew all about the conscious policies of a foundation and the qualities of its officers, it would nevertheless be rash to dogmatize about it, and for the following reason. Many an author has recorded that at a certain stage in the writing of a novel the characters seem to develop a will and a personality of their own, and from that point on the story writes itself. In just the same way the program of a foundation in any field sometimes seems to take on a will of its own, and the power of decision which its trustees are supposed to wield becomes rather an illusory thing.

The Foundation

When Mr. Carnegie and Mr. Rockefeller and the others set up the endowments and foundations which bear their names, they were, I am sure, thinking of them solely as agencies for the distribution of the wealth for which, in Mr. Carnegie's term, they were "stewards," and had no realization that these bodies would in time come to serve other purposes. More and more, however, they have become clearing houses of ideas, and are today among the best places to find out what thoughtful men and women regard as the things of chief moment for the present and for the future. Such a service has been performed in the recent publication by the Carnegie Foundation on college athletics. Much of what one university learns about another is learned in foundation offices. In appraising the usefulness of the foundation, considerable weight should be given to this by-product. The foundation may also have another useful function to perform when plain speaking is needed. As an unbiased critic, competent to speak with authority, it may perform a service of outstanding importance. Among incidental by-products of foundation activity may be mentioned the lessons they teach through their refusal to consider proposals that have not been thought out upon a reasonable budgetary basis.

The opportunities open to foundations will be constantly changing, both as to fields of activity and as to methods of operation. Let us take education as an example. A few years ago, perhaps the most useful form of foundation help lay in the financing of impartial fact-finding surveys. The survey is today just as useful as ever, but other agencies, including cities, States, and the Federal Government, are now educated to the point of meeting the necessary expenses and of engaging competent professional direction. Once the value to humanity of any line of activity becomes clearly established, as, for example, it has become established in medical research, foundation contributions become relatively less necessary.

I think the tendency of the foundation to seek its own opportunities rather than merely to decide among those which come to its attention will grow more marked. Just as the astronomer in his observatory will naturally turn his telescope to those parts of the heavens of which we know the least, a foundation will attempt to search out the bare spots in human knowledge. It must seek opportunities in the uncultivated areas lying between the normal, radial lines of progress. For example, the school library lies between the special fields of the teacher and the librarian. Sometimes an entire realm of neglected opportunity can be found, such as existed only a very few years ago in adult education. The foundation must also, I think, be sensitive to recognize such regions of unrest as may be found in the fine arts today. One can trace a growing tendency to insist less and less on clean-cut proposals, and a growing willingness to undertake what might be called speculative ventures. Provided the general objective is recognized to be of importance and timeliness, measurability of results is regarded as of secondary importance.

I look forward to seeing the foundations continue their present close relationships with colleges and universities, but on an ever-changing basis as to specific objectives and plans of operation. Take, for example, the place of the college in the community in which it is situated. The old monastic conception, with the separa-

Conclusion

tion of town and gown and the incessant conflict between them, has been completely obliterated in the march of modern life, but people behave as if it still existed. This is so much the case that the colleges which are now recognizing the possibility of intellectual service outside the classroom, even to their own alumni, are actually regarded as daring pioneers.

In the whole realm of various and often conflicting movements, which we roughly group together as progressive education, there will be real opportunities for the foundations to be of service. These won't be easy to find, it is true, because the movement has its characteristic lunatic fringe, and the loud speakers constantly in operation make it particularly difficult to catch the still, small voices. In the general diffusion of knowledge and particularly of recently acquired knowledge we are accumulating the new information far more rapidly than we are making it available outside the classroom. What the English call "vulgarization" is being admirably done in a few subjects, but in many of the others the old fallacy that popularization is in some way an undignified activity for a scholar still persists, and the subject remains without its Huxley.

From the early ages until the time of our grandfathers, there was practically no change in the technical methods by which ideas are communicated from one human mind to another, except the invention of printing. Since photography, however, there has been a steady procession of fundamental inventions which have developed much more rapidly than has the power of education to apply them. The moving-picture was permitted to become thoroughly commercialized before any foundation asked itself the question, "Is there any way in which we can help this new instrument of human communication to further the purposes for which we stand?" It is, I think, significant that today the foundations are studying the corresponding problems presented by the radio, a little late, it is true, but not, I think, too late.

There are also techniques in human conduct and procedure which may prove to be of great importance in the exchange of ideas and which need the kind of continuous study and experimentation which is seldom, if ever, possible without foundation help. As an example of what I have in mind, I might cite one which is already receiving such aid. At the recent meeting of the Institute of Pacific Relations at Kyoto, the customary type of program, with its formal papers and its parliamentary procedure, was abandoned in favor of a new kind of group discussion, based on carefully guided preliminary preparation. The results were far from conclusive, but were sufficiently encouraging to justify further effort.

Few would deny that amid all the cross currents and confusions of modern life, the outstanding human aspiration today is for peace among men. We are really living in a peace-loving world, but a world which doesn't believe that peace can be maintained by preaching about the evils of war. It is a world which is beginning to realize that wars don't happen from spontaneous combustion—wars start from little hot points, and if we really understood what our neighbors were thinking about and particularly what they were feeling, these hot points could be recognized and attended to before they develop high temperatures and ten-sion, and finally cause a state of national hysteria when it's too late to do anything but fight. I question whether the present trend toward the international in foundation programs is the result of deliberate decision, but I am sure it is significant, and I expect to see it continue upon an expanding scale. Science, letters and the arts know no national boundaries, and in the world-wide pattern of scientific research, we already see the Rockefeller Foundation supporting locally conducted researches in Australia and the Carnegie Corporation in South Africa. Even more important, however, is the growth of opportunity to individuals through traveling fellowships. The late Rector of the Sorbonne, Dr. Paul Lapie, stated shortly before his death that in his judgment the outstanding social phenomenon of the years following the war had been the renewal of the scholarly migrations which were the outstanding feature of the life of the Middle Ages and the Renaissance. The degree to which foundations have already aided in these international migrations is very striking. The officials of the Rockefeller Foundation and the General Education Board have been kind enough to check

Conclusion

up their programs for fellowships and visiting professorships, and have come to the following astonishing total:

These two foundations have given appointments to no fewer than 5,827 individuals at a cost of almost exactly nine and a half million dollars. The program of a single year, 1929, includes 1,451 such appointments.

Although the Rockefeller contribution is by far the largest, there are nine other agencies active in this field whose reports are available, and their records show, again for a typical year, 600 appointments at a total cost of $1,069,300. These do not all involve foreign travel or residence, but this is true in the majority of cases.

In our look toward the future, we must consider not only the opportunities open to the foundations, but the possibilities of danger. Some of the early fears have proved quite unfounded, as, for example, the fear that foundation aid would dry up the springs of individual philanthropy. Quite the contrary has proved to be the case. Nor do we hear today the expressions of alarm voiced, as you will recall, in the

Congressional Report of 1916 that "the domination by the men in whose hands the final control of a large part of American industry rests . . . is being extended largely through the creation of enormous privately managed funds for indefinite purposes. . . . The funds of these foundations are largely invested in securities of corporations. . . . The policies of these foundations must inevitably be colored, if not controlled, to conform to the policies of such corporations." Today any one of twenty life insurance companies or any one of a hundred banks has larger sums at its disposal than the aggregate resources of the foundations, even assuming that the latter should share the same ideas as to how their funds should be spent, which thus far they have never done.

We must not forget, however, that earlier foundations, notably some of the English Guilds, did actually degenerate, both as to the custody of capital and the use of income. I doubt whether we need worry particularly as to the former. Our community standards as regards finance are distinctly higher today. Accountancy has become a profession, and public opinion demands at least an annual audit. As to the use of funds available for the stated purposes of the trust, that is and should be a constant cause, not for worry, but for thought on the part of those directly concerned and a fair field of criticism on the part of those outside. It is to ensure this criticism that I have insisted, I fear to the point of being wearisome, upon the fullest publicity regarding foundation activities.

I confess I haven't so ready an answer to one other problem. We all know that foundation aid can increase measurably the pace of any social tendency, but we don't know when this artificial acceleration ceases to be desirable, or even becomes one of those "social toxins," to use Dr. Pritchett's phrase, "which do enough harm to more than counteract the benefit that may come from the original gift." All I can say is that here as elsewhere safety lies in the fullest available information as to foundation affairs and the widest possible discussion regarding them.

The question is often asked as to whether foundations will increase in number, and whether this is desirable. Personally I think it is very desirable, provided the donor is willing to take advice and to profit by the experience of others. I doubt whether we shall ever have a greater need for the disinterested search for truth to guide us in the rapidly shifting conditions of social and economic life, nor will there be available a wider economic leeway to justify the setting aside of the funds for the purpose. Last year there were 496 persons taxed on incomes of one million dollars or more, and there were twenty-four in the five million income class.

My own feeling is that we shall see few, if any, new foundations of very large size, say $100,000,000 or over, but that there will be a steady increase in those of somewhat smaller size, say from $3,000,000 to $15,000,000 in capitalization (within which figures would fall the existing Russell Sage, Milbank, and Guggenheim Foundations). The present foundations, though all young in years, have come to have traditional obligations in certain fields, and all are overloaded with opportunities to spend money for the further development of enterprises already begun. It is indeed grow-

Conclusion

ing increasingly difficult, even by informal understanding among existing trusts, to make provision to give adequate help to new undertakings outside the existing programs. I have set down elsewhere a list of needed foundations. The series includes studies in rural life, recreation, the home and family, the church as a social agency, museums and parks, town and regional planning, housing, technical training below the college level, nursing, and dental education. Perhaps, though the enterprise would be fraught with danger, the greatest single contribution which could be made to human progress would be the discovery of means for the early recognition of what we call genius.

If the sums actually devoted each year to the creation of foundations were applied to these purposes, they would soon meet the existing needs. During 1927-28 more than ninety-three million dollars was added to the total of foundation funds, without counting either foundation gifts to universities and hospitals, nor the Huntington and Cranbrook Foundations, both special in character. As one looks over the announcements of foundations established in recent years, however, one finds the greater number devoted to enterprises which, while generous in purpose, are palliative rather than constructive in character. The best we can do at present is to look forward hopefully to the time when men and women will deliberately seek the most-needed activity. An example of what may be done as a result of intelligent study may be found in the basic program of the new Spelman Fund, which will be devoted to establishing effective contacts between the theoretical and the practical in public administration. Only last week a new foundation was organized, upon what seems to me an admirable plan, evidently the result of careful preliminary study. This is the Josiah Macy, Jr., Memorial, for medical research and the prevention and cure of disease.

As believers in democracy, we are bound to look forward to the day when the community will take over the functions now performed by the foundations of the type we have discussed, and the latter will accordingly disappear or, at any rate, become a factor of relatively slight importance. If we are honest with ourselves, however, we must recognize that

Conclusion

that day will not come in our time nor in that of our children or grandchildren.

In these lectures I have attempted to give some idea of the different types of American foundations, and something of the background from which they developed. I have told of the birth of the Carnegie and Rockefeller groups, and the welcome they received. If the question of foundation policy has not been clarified, some indication of its complexity has been given. A discussion of the organization and procedure of typical foundations has followed, with some examples of foundation activities. Then an imaginary donor has been evoked, for the purpose of giving him some good advice; the influence of human personality has been touched upon; and finally you have had one man's guess as to the trend of future developments.

Throughout, I have tried to answer a good many questions, and I hope I have stirred up a good many more in your own minds. If I have left the general impression that those who are concerned with these American foundations are satisfied with what they have accomplished,

I shall have missed my purpose. We cannot minimize and we do not wish to minimize the number and gravity of our errors, of emphasis, of selection, and of performance. After all, the foundation has shared the limitations of all human organizations, whether they be religious or political or social, and is no more entitled than any of the others to self-satisfaction. If, however, its limitations are those of common humanity, so also are its opportunities, and I should equally have missed my purpose if I have failed to make clear my firm conviction that with all their shortcomings the net accomplishment of these foundations justifies their acceptance by the community as instruments with no longer an experimental but a permanent place in the order of things. Let me close as I closed a discussion at a university gathering some years ago, as follows:

The foundations make mistakes, both of omission and of commission, in this imperfect world, and they will continue to do so. The real test of their utility lies in their record of positive accomplishment. I shall give just two examples of such accomplishment. In the first place, no history of American education would

Conclusion

be complete without recognition of the responsibility of the General Education Board for the improvement of secondary education all through our Southern States. Secondly, the story of human progress through the quarter century just closing could not be told, no matter how briefly, without reference to what the Rockefeller Foundation has done for public health throughout the world.

At the time, I purposely omitted the development of the American public library, as resulting too directly from the personal gifts of Andrew Carnegie. Perhaps my attitude today is less technical. At any rate, I feel now that this piece of evidence should be added to the two others and that upon the three the foundations may safely rest their case.